Dear Parent:

P9-BZH-327

Congratulations! Your child is taking
the first steps on an exciting journey.
The destination? Independent reading!

STEP INTO READING® will help your child get there. The program offers
five steps to reading success. Each step includes fun stories and colorful art.
There are also Step into Reading Sticker Books, Step into Reading Math
Readers, Step into Reading Write-In Readers, Step into Reading Phonics
Readers, and Step into Reading Phonics First Steps! Boxed Sets—a complete
literacy program with something for every child.

Learning to Read, Step by Step!

Ready to Read   Preschool–Kindergarten
• **big type and easy words** • **rhyme and rhythm** • **picture clues**
For children who know the alphabet and are eager to
begin reading.

Reading with Help   Preschool–Grade 1
• **basic vocabulary** • **short sentences** • **simple stories**
For children who recognize familiar words and sound out
new words with help.

Reading on Your Own   Grades 1–3
• **engaging characters** • **easy-to-follow plots** • **popular topics**
For children who are ready to read on their own.

Reading Paragraphs   Grades 2–3
• **challenging vocabulary** • **short paragraphs** • **exciting stories**
For newly independent readers who read simple sentences
with confidence.

Ready for Chapters   Grades 2–4
• **chapters** • **longer paragraphs** • **full-color art**
For children who want to take the plunge into chapter books
but still like colorful pictures.

STEP INTO READING® is designed to give every child a successful
reading experience. The grade levels are only guides. Children can progress
through the steps at their own speed, developing confidence in their
reading, no matter what their grade.

Remember, a lifetime love of reading starts with a single step!

For Megan—M.D.

For Rebecca, Wynn, and Parks—B.B.

The author and editor would like to thank Gregory Curtis, author of *The Cave Painters,* for his assistance in the preparation of this book.

Text copyright © 2010 by Mark Dubowski
Illustrations copyright © 2010 by Bryn Barnard

All rights reserved.
Published in the United States by Random House Children's Books,
a division of Random House, Inc., New York.

Step into Reading, Random House, and the Random House colophon are registered trademarks of Random House, Inc.

Visit us on the Web!
www.stepintoreading.com

Educators and librarians, for a variety of teaching tools, visit us at
www.randomhouse.com/teachers

Library of Congress Cataloging-in-Publication Data
Dubowski, Mark.
Discovery in the cave / by Mark Dubowski ; illustrated by Bryn Barnard.
  p. cm. — (Step into reading ; Step 4)
ISBN 978-0-375-85893-2 (pbk.) — ISBN 978-0-375-95893-9 (lib. bdg.)
1. Magdalenian culture—France—Montignac (Dordogne)—Juvenile literature. 2. Cave paintings—France—Montignac (Dordogne)—Juvenile literature. 3. Art, Prehistoric—France—Montignac (Dordogne)—Juvenile literature. 4. Montignac (Dordogne, France)—Antiquities—Juvenile literature. [1. Lascaux Cave (France)—Juvenile literature.] I. Barnard, Bryn. II. Title.
GN772.3.M3D83 2010
944'.72—dc22   2009007099

Printed in the United States of America
10 9 8 7 6 5 4 3 2 1

Random House Children's Books supports the First Amendment and celebrates the right to read.

STEP INTO READING®

STEP 4

Discovery in the Cave

by Mark Dubowski

illustrated by Bryn Barnard

Random House 🏠 New York

CHAPTER 1
Earthquake

A bison climbs down a mound of rock. It is night, when bison should be sleeping. But tonight, something is wrong. There are sounds like thunder coming from inside the mountain.

At the top of the mountain, a rock comes loose and tumbles down. It smashes into other rocks, breaking them apart. Then another one falls. And another. Suddenly it looks as if the whole mountain is going to shake itself apart.

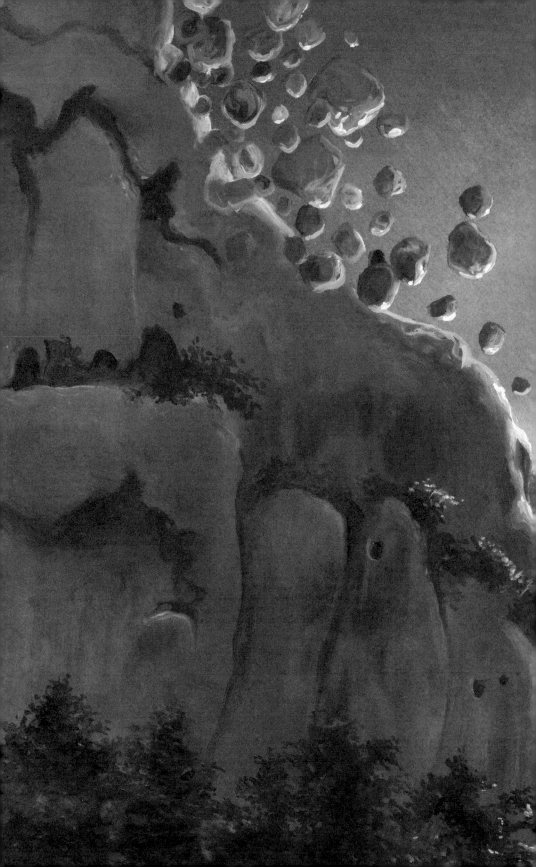

It is an earthquake. The bison springs down the mountain, chased by boulders and stones and gravel that falls like hard rain. The frightened animal barely gets away before one whole side of the mountain breaks apart and slides downhill!

Seconds later, it is over. The mountain is quiet, but it has changed. Rocks that were at the top are now piled up at the bottom. Trees are bent and broken.

In one place, the entrance to a cave has been buried under rubble.

Was anyone inside?

No one will know the answer for thousands of years.

CHAPTER 2
Discovery!

"Robot!" someone shouts.

A dog barks. His name is Robot. The person who called him is Marcel Ravidat. He is seventeen years old. Marcel and Robot are in a forest near Marcel's home in France. The boy and the dog have been here before, hunting rabbits. Today, they are hunting for something else.

It is September 12, 1940. Marcel and Robot have come to the forest with three of Marcel's friends. Marcel wants to show them something Robot found when they were hunting.

The boys catch up with Robot. They are at the trunk of a large tree that has fallen to the ground. The roots of the tree are torn from the soil. Where the tree stood, there is now a deep hole. But the hole is deeper than the roots of the tree.

The boys dig to make the hole bigger. Marcel thinks it might hold buried treasure! "That's enough digging," says Marcel. He holds something—a tool from his uncle's garage. A grease gun. Marcel strikes a match and holds the flame to the tip of the gun. The grease catches fire and burns like a candle.

Then Marcel disappears down the hole!

Robot whines. Where is Marcel? The
other boys look into the hole.

"Come on!" Marcel is standing in the
light of the torch, ten feet down. Marcel's
friends tumble in after him!

The hole is dark and cool. At the bottom is a tunnel, with walls made of clay. The tunnel does not go straight down, but it is steep. Marcel leads the way. The four boys are walking underground, deep beneath the forest.

After a while, the walls of the tunnel change. Instead of clay, they are now made of limestone, a kind of rock. The path becomes less steep. Then they are out of the tunnel—and inside a cave!

The floor is slippery and wet. The boys watch their step. Marcel notices something strange. Above their heads, the walls of the cave are covered with calcite, a bright white mineral. Marcel lifts his torch, looks up, and gets a big surprise.

Someone was here before them!

Above their heads, the white walls of the cave are decorated with large paintings of animals. Horses. Stags with horns as big as tree branches. Huge animals that look like oxen.

Some are standing. Others look as if they are running through the cave, charging along the edge of a high cliff.

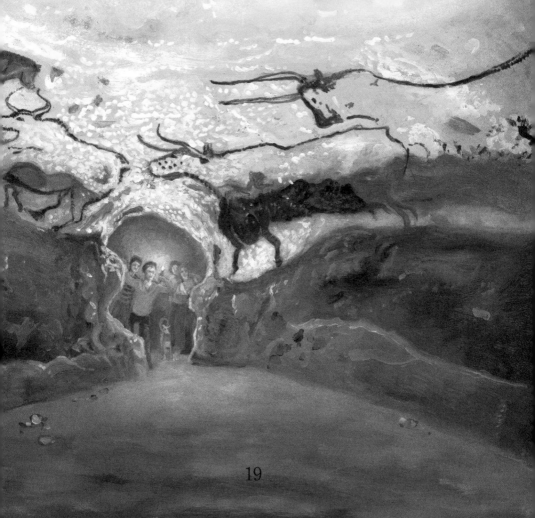

Outside, a warplane crosses the sky. It is a German Messerschmitt. France is at war. Enemy soldiers have moved into many French cities.

When the boys come out of the cave, they are worried. For now, the cave is theirs. They found it. What will happen if other people find out about it?

But they are also excited. A secret like
this is hard to keep. They think of one
person they can trust. Someone who knows
a lot about old caves. Monsieur Léon Laval.

Monsieur Laval is their former science teacher. The boys talk to him. They take him to the cave.

Monsieur Laval has seen cave paintings before. But not like these.

"Look at the way the animals are drawn," he tells the boys. The faces are turned slightly, to make the paintings look less flat and more real. Some of the animals are carefully drawn over bulges in the rock wall that are shaped like the animals' bodies.

On the floor, they find chips of animal bone and rock powder that was used to make paint.

The things they find, and the paintings, are very old.

CHAPTER 3
16,000 BC

A man wearing animal hide walks up a mountain trail. The trail follows the path of a dry riverbed. Many years before the man was born, water ran here.

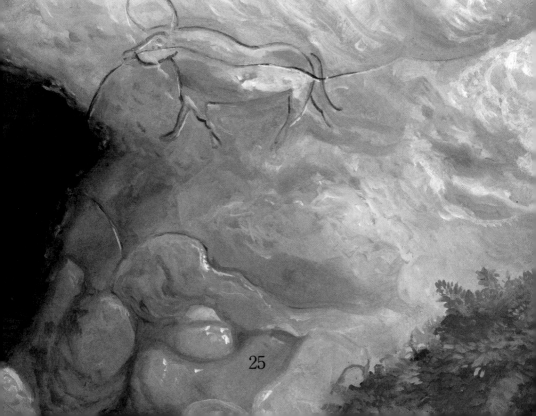

The water ran right through the mountain and formed a cave. The shells of clams and mussels living in the water stained the walls of the cave white. Then the river dried up and left an empty cave.

The man walks into the cave. He carries a hollowed-out stone holding animal fat. The fat is burning, making a kind of candle. It lights the way.

The man is an artist. He has come here to paint.

Inside the cave are other artists. They have built a scaffold—a platform made of wood.

The man climbs the scaffold to reach the top of the cave, where the wall is most white. He mixes powdered rock with water to make paint. He carefully spreads the paint onto the wall with a rag made of animal hide.

Other artists have been here before. Their paintings are on the wall, too. The man is careful not to paint over the older artwork. To the herd of horses that was already painted there, he adds another one. A red pony with a black head.

CHAPTER 4
Famous

Monsieur Laval writes a letter to Henri Breuil. Breuil is a priest and an expert on prehistoric art. "Come to Lascaux," writes Laval.

Breuil comes. He has seen cave art all over the world. But these pictures are the best he has ever seen.

He tells the boys about the oxen. "They are aurochs," he says. "They are extinct—they no longer exist. But they are the great-grandparents of all cows and bulls living today."

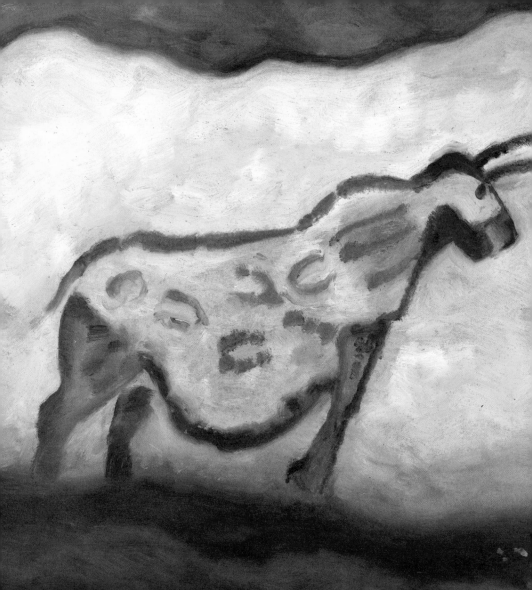

One animal puzzles even Breuil. It looks like an aurochs, but its horns are too straight and too long. Its legs are too thick. What could it be?

Maybe it is an imaginary animal—not real, like a unicorn. Or maybe it is not an animal at all. The thick legs could belong to a hunter. He could be playing a trick, hiding under an animal's skin.

The big room that the boys first discovered is only the beginning. The cave at Lascaux turns out to have five rooms of paintings.

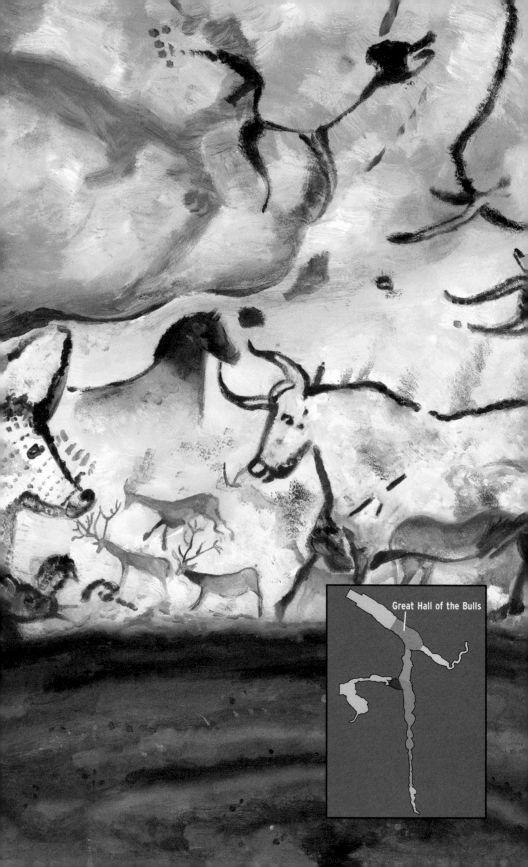

Great Hall of the Bulls

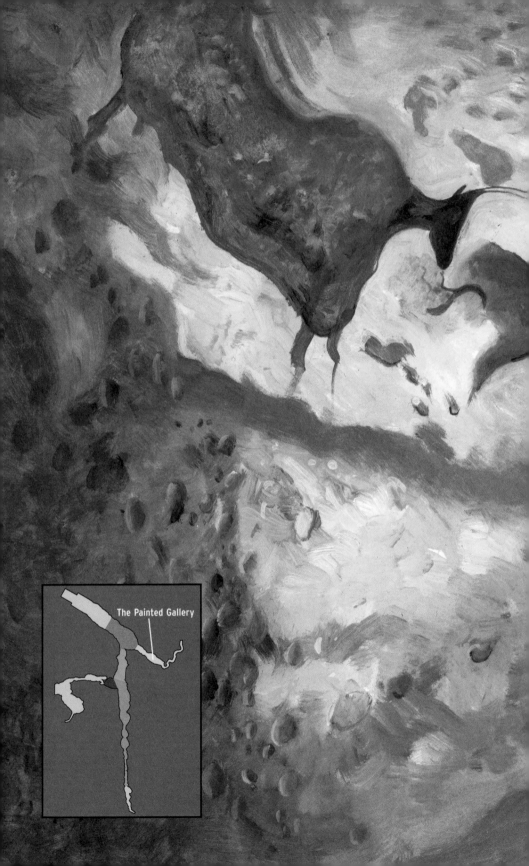

The Painted Gallery

Through a keyhole-shaped tunnel at the other end is another room. Here the paintings cover the walls and the ceiling.

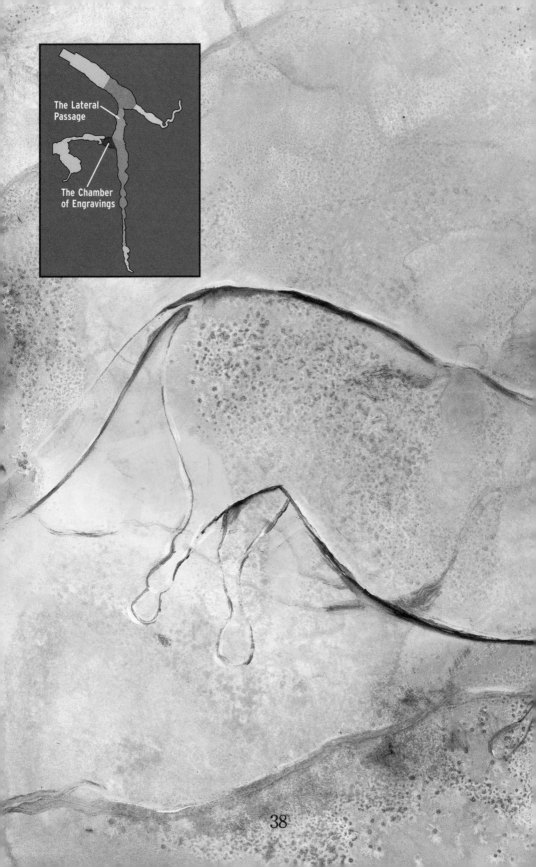

The Lateral
Passage

The Chamber
of Engravings

38

In the next tunnel, the paintings are faded, probably from water seeping into the cave long ago.

The tunnel leads to a room with more than six hundred paintings and a thousand engravings—drawings scratched into the rock. They cover the walls and ceiling.

The next room has five painted scenes. This one shows a black cow standing in front of horses, bison, and ibexes. An ibex is a kind of wild goat with large horns.

The Main Gallery

After that is a room that has a different animal. It is a kind of large cat, or "feline." It looks something like a cave lion, or jaguar. The European jaguar is long extinct.

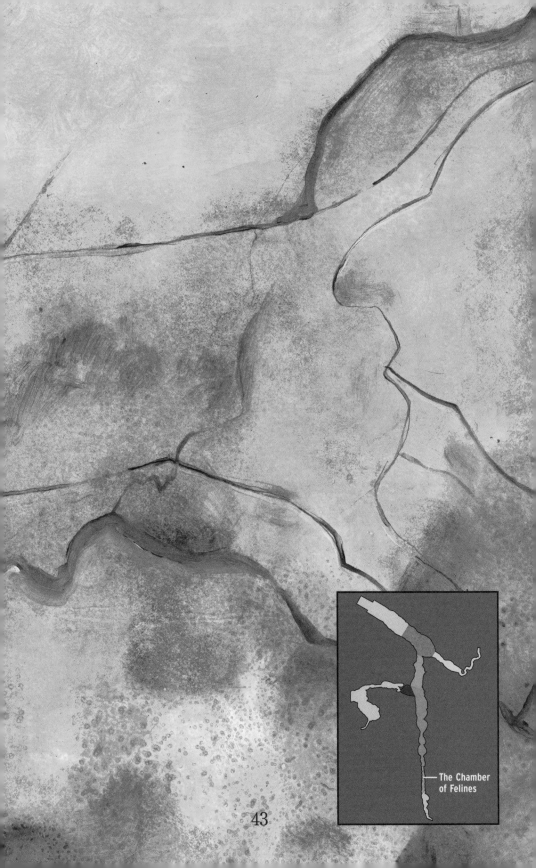

The Chamber
of Felines

Breuil tells other experts about the cave. They come from all over the world to see it. Before long, the cave at Lascaux is famous.

Over the years, the cave is changed. Men build a smooth path inside. They put in electric lights. They add a door to the entrance. They put in machines that control the air in the cave.

Many visitors come to see the cave.
Soon, over a thousand people walk through
it every day. The cave is like a museum.
It even has guards.
One of them is a man named Marcel
Ravidat.

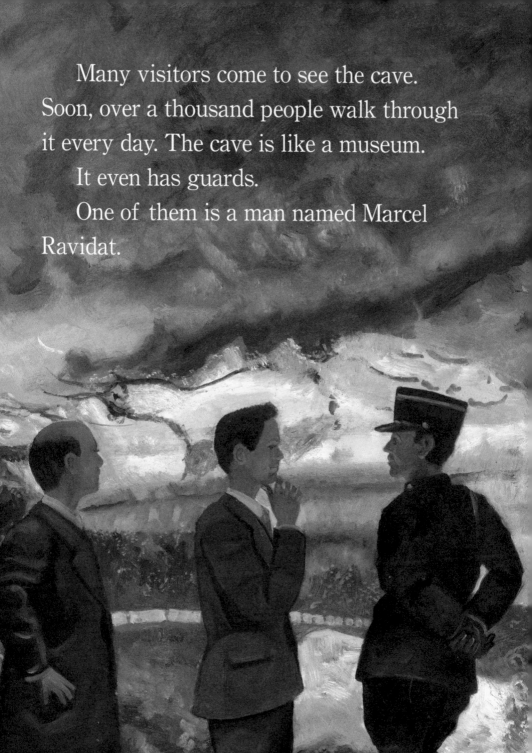

Author's Note

In 1963, the cave at Lascaux was closed to visitors. Exposed to air and light, the paintings were fading. Now visitors enter a model—a life-size copy of the front of the cave. Partly underground, it is made of cement. The walls are shaped exactly like the walls of the real cave and decorated with exact copies of the paintings.

In the real cave, the paintings are back in the dark, the way they were for thousands of years—before they were found by four boys and a dog.